# CONSERVING RAIN FORESTS

Martin Banks

STECK-VAUGHN
LIBRARY

*Austin, Texas*

# Conserving Our World

**Acid Rain**
**Conserving Rain Forests**
**Waste and Recycling**
**Conserving the Atmosphere**
**Protecting Wildlife**
**The Spread of Deserts**

**Cover:** An area of rain forest in the
Genting Highlands of Malaysia.

**Series editor:** Sue Hadden
**Series designer:** Ross George

**First published in the United States in 1990 by
Steck-Vaughn Co., Austin, Texas,** a subsidiary of National
Education Corporation.

First published in 1989 by Wayland (Publishers) Ltd.
© Copyright 1989 Wayland (Publishers) Ltd

**Library of Congress Cataloging-in Publication Data**

Banks, Martin, 1947–
   Conserving rain forests

   (Conserving our world)
   Includes bibliographical references.
   Summary: Describes the rapidity with which the rain
forests of the world are being destroyed, the harm to
plants, animals, and humans, and remedies for preserving
the rain forests.
   1. Rain forest ecology—Juvenile literature,   2. Forest
conservation—Juvenile literature.   [1. Rain forest
ecology.   2. Forest conservation.   3. Ecology]   I. Title.
II. Series
QH541.4.R27B36   1990         574-5'2642         89-21658
ISBN 0-8114-2387-5

Printed in Italy
Bound in the United States

   2 3 4 5 6 7 8 9 0 Sa 94 93 92 91 90

# Contents

Some years ago I was part of a group visiting the hills of southwest India to search for a rare species of monkey that lives in the tropical rain forest there. As we entered the forest, the sunlight faded because it was filtered through the dense foliage. We found ourselves in an area dominated by enormous small-leaved evergreen trees, their trunks festooned with creepers and vines. Beneath them grew a layer of shrubs and ferns, among which darted brightly colored butterflies and birds such as flycatchers.

We were hoping to see the wanderoo, a rare Southeast Asian macaque. We spent hours slowly walking through the dense forest, peering into the dimly lit upper branches of the trees, where we knew the monkeys could be found. Finally we located some and were able to watch them at close quarters as they fed and moved through the trees. The troop of monkeys was large and contained many young. They would be safe for the future, we thought, as this forest was part of a protected wildlife sanctuary.

*Rain forests are among the richest habitats in the world. They contain an incredible diversity of animal life, including many tree-dwelling mammals like this squirrel monkey from South America.*

*Some rain forests have already been completely destroyed, along with all their animal life.*

Eventually the troop of monkeys moved out of sight and we walked on to the edge of the forest. We emerged in brilliant sunshine to a scene of utter devastation. As far as the eye could see in any direction, the ground was bare of trees, covered in the roots and stumps of trees that had been felled. Enormous stacks of timber were piled high, awaiting transportation. A few tall isolated trees still stood overlooking the destruction all around them.

Not so long ago, the whole area before us had no doubt been covered in rain forest. The lower slopes of the hillsides had been the first to be cleared to create tea plantations. Now the higher forests were being cleared, too, leaving only small pockets of rain forest. Later we discovered that,

despite being a wildlife sanctuary, the rain forest we had visited covered an area of less than one square mile. We were left to wonder sadly how long the monkeys, and all the other plants and animals we had seen, could continue to survive in their very small patch of rain forest in southwest India.

The account you have just read concerned the Indian rain forest, but very similar stories could be told about rain forest areas of Africa, South America, and Southeast Asia. All the world's rain forests are under great threat of destruction and their future survival is in doubt. This book will explain why the rain forests are in such danger and what can be done to save them before it is too late.

*There are many different types of rain forests. This photograph shows the astounding variety of trees that grow in the equatorial rain forests. The photograph was taken in Ecuador, a country that was named after the Equator.*

## What is a rain forest?

Rain forests are one of the richest and most diverse habitats that still exist in the world today. They are found at both temperate and tropical latitudes of the earth, but tropical rain forest, which is found closer to the Equator, contains the most plant and animal life.

The earliest record we have that describes the appearance and atmosphere of a rain forest is that of the explorer, Christopher Columbus. In his voyages of discovery around the world, he opened up new trade and shipping routes. Columbus is best remembered for his journey to the Americas, but he was also the first European to locate the West Indies. In 1492 Columbus landed on the mountainous island of Haiti. Entering its rain forest, he beautifully described the sights and sounds that greeted him:

"I never beheld so fair a thing; trees beautiful and green and different from ours, with flowers and fruits each according to their kind, many and little birds which sing very sweetly."

Four centuries after Columbus' arrival, a German botanist gave these forests their modern name "rain forest." The many travelers and scientists who had visited them in between referred to them simply as forests or tropical forests. While many of them marveled at the abundance of animals and plants they contained, it is only more recently that we have begun to realize just how exceptional and unique a rain forest really is.

What exactly is a tropical rain forest, and how does it differ from other forests? There are many different types of rain forests. Some botanists recognize thirty or more, including evergreen forests, semideciduous forests, cloud forests at high altitudes on mountains, and lowland forests that grow along the banks of rivers. We can distinguish two main types. First, equatorial rain forests grow close to the Equator and experience very high temperatures and rainfall. The trees in these forests are mainly evergreens, and there is little variation in the seasons of the year. Second, at a distance away from the Equator, lower temperatures and rainfall combine with more variable seasons to produce a different rain forest type. The forests here are termed "moist" or "semideciduous." They do not have quite the same abundance of plants and animals as equatorial rain forests.

Many people assume that a rain forest is what is popularly referred to as a jungle. To most of us, the word jungle conjures up the image of a very dense growth of tall grass, shrubs, and trees, full of trailing creepers and an assortment of noisy and dangerous animals. Jungles are thought of as impenetrable to all but the most fearless explorer, armed with a sharp machete.

In fact, a tropical rain forest bears little relation to our notions of the jungle. It has clearly defined layers of vegetation. The crowns of the tall rain forest trees form a dense, leafy layer called the canopy. At a much lower level grow bushes and shrubs that form what is called the understory. In Equatorial rain forests, the dense canopy excludes all but a few shafts of sunlight so that the understory contains relatively little vegetation, while the forest floor consists of bare earth carpeted with leaves and rotting vegetation.

*Rain forests are found at high altitudes right down to sea level, as here in Surinam.*

*The ground level of this Javan rain forest is a thick tangle of vines and creepers.*

Beneath the trees in the rain forest it is quiet and dim. Though animals are abundant, they are seldom seen or heard. Strange bird calls disturb the still air occasionally, while a crashing of branches high up in the treetops gives away the presence of a troop of monkeys or a giant squirrel. A flock of gaily colored parrots, or a group of brightly patterned butterflies bring sudden life to a quiet sunlit clearing. But the atmosphere of the rain forest is really more like that of a dimly lit cathedral than a jungle.

## Where are the rain forests?

Tropical rain forest is the natural vegetation of the lands that lie along the Equator, between the Tropics of Cancer to the North and Capricorn to the South. The main requirements for the growth of rain forest are a heavy annual rainfall, of at least 100 inches a year, together with a high average temperature of around 80°F. Farther away from the Equator, rainfall of about 80 inches per year and fluctuating temperatures produce the semideciduous type of forest.

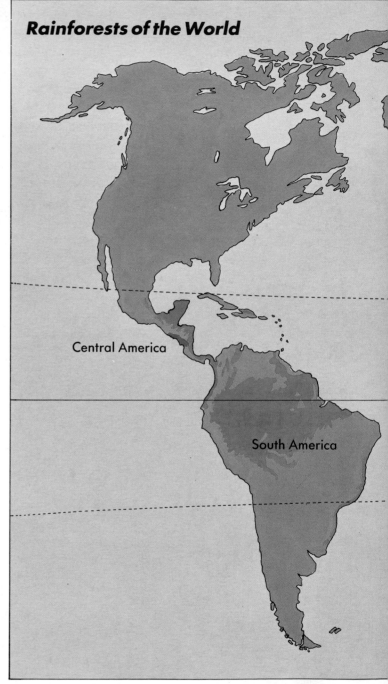

**Rainforests of the World**

Central America

South America

Many millions of years ago, when the climate of the earth was much warmer, rain forests extended across much of the world, far to the north and south of their current regions. Pollen grains of rain forest plants have been discovered in places as far north as London and even in Alaska. So rain

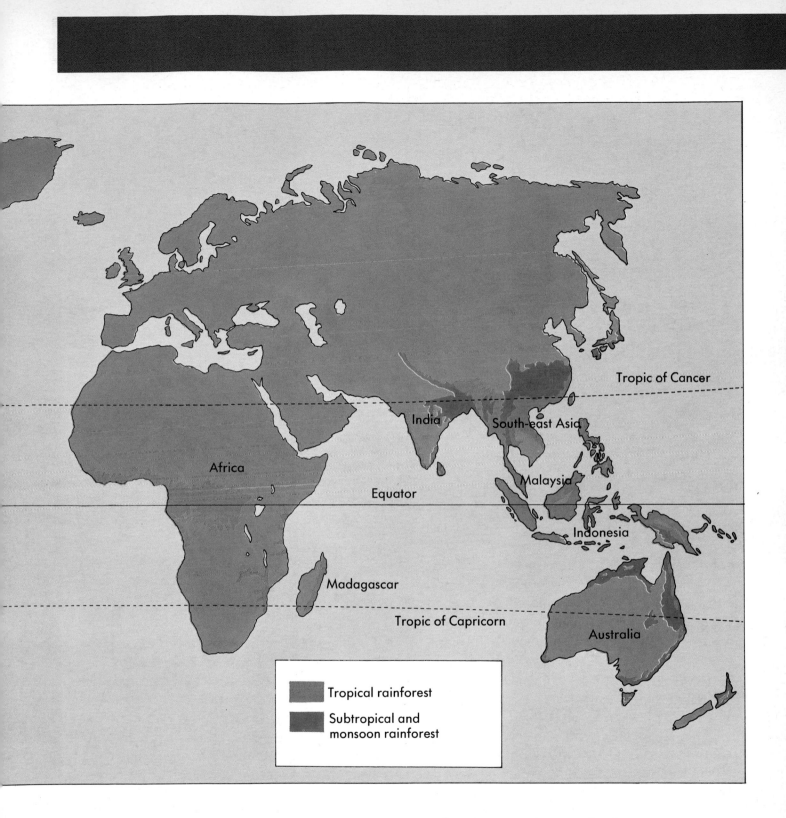

Tropic of Cancer

India

South-east Asia

Africa

Malaysia

Equator

Indonesia

Madagascar

Tropic of Capricorn

Australia

Tropical rainforest

Subtropical and
monsoon rainforest

forest represents one of the most ancient, or primeval, natural habitats of the world. Just a few thousand years ago, 14 percent of the earth's land surface was covered by rain forest of one type or another. Within the last two hundred years, over half that area has been converted into pasture, farmland, or simply wasteland.

Today rain forests are only found in South and Central America, central Africa, the island of Madagascar in the Indian Ocean, and in Southeast Asia. The Asian forests are found from India through Malaysia and the Philippines to northern

Australia. The largest areas of existing rain forest are in South and Central America. The vast basin of the Amazon River and its tributaries contains over half of the rain forests left in the world. The rain forests of Amazonia represent the greatest unspoiled areas of tropical rain forest left in the world today, and harbor an enormous wealth of plant and animal life. Brazil alone contains a third of the remaining rain forests. Also in Brazil, there are the last small remnants of a once extensive rain forest that stretched along the Atlantic coast. This area contains some of the rarest species of monkeys left in the world.

Across the Atlantic Ocean, the rain forests of the Congo basin in central Africa have a similar appearance to those of the New World. The

*The largest remaining areas of rain forest are in South and Central America, mostly in the Amazon basin and Brazil, which has a third of all rain forest left in the world.*

animals and plants here, however, are quite different from their counterparts which live in the forests of the New World. The forests of Madagascar, which split off from the mainland of Africa millions of years ago, contain a quite different assortment of flora and fauna from the rain forests of central Africa.

Rain forests are also found in a number of different countries in Southeast Asia, from the northeastern tip of Australia to southern China. Thousands of islands, large and small, make up the country collectively called Indonesia. The larger islands of Borneo, Sumatra, Java, and New Guinea all have rain forests, too. All together, Southeast Asia contains about a quarter of the world's remaining rain forests.

Each of the three main rain forest areas are separated from one another by thousands of miles of ocean and they each contain their own unique plants and animals. The forests have not always been isolated in this way. Originally, the land masses on which they are found were joined together. When the continents split apart long ago, most of the flora and fauna of each developed differently. However, a few species of rain forest plants and animals inhabit more than one of the main areas, and a handful actually occur in all three. This is rather conclusive evidence of the fact that all the rain forests originally lay within a continuous land mass. (See also diagram below.)

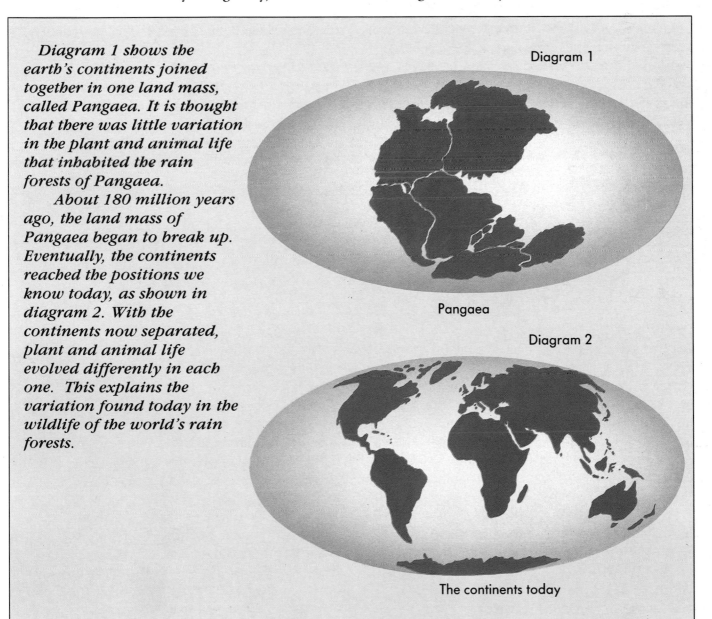

*Diagram 1 shows the earth's continents joined together in one land mass, called Pangaea. It is thought that there was little variation in the plant and animal life that inhabited the rain forests of Pangaea.*

*About 180 million years ago, the land mass of Pangaea began to break up. Eventually, the continents reached the positions we know today, as shown in diagram 2. With the continents now separated, plant and animal life evolved differently in each one. This explains the variation found today in the wildlife of the world's rain forests.*

Diagram 1

Pangaea

Diagram 2

The continents today

# The Structure of a Rain Forest

As we have read, a tropical rain forest consists of several distinct layers. The explorer Alexander von Humboldt called it "a forest above a forest." Each of these layers creates a separate habitat for the animals and plants that live there. So a rain forest actually supports several quite different plant and animal communities.

The top layer of the rain forest is created by the canopy. The tall trees mostly reach a height of between 100 and 200 feet. Their trunks are normally smooth for most of this height, only branching out to form the crown at the limit of their growth. The crown of each tree almost touches the next, forming a mass of leaves and branches that prevents the sunlight from reaching the lower layers. A few trees grow much higher than others, pushing up through the level of the canopy. These giants of the forest, with their crowns standing high above the rest, are called emergents.

The second layer of the rain forest is often called the understory. It consists of shrubs, ferns and small trees that are able to thrive in the dimly lit dampness below the canopy. Ferns and palms have long thin leaves to help them absorb the little sunlight that filters down from the canopy. In rain forests near the Equator, many of the trees are evergreen and so form a canopy that blots out the sun throughout the year. The understory of

*The diagram below illustrates the vegetation layers typically found in rain forests. The vegetation of the understory is very sparse in Equatorial rain forests.*

emergent layer

canopy

lianas

understory

forest floor

these particular forests is extremely sparse.

The forest floor forms the lowest layer of the rain forest. The ground is carpeted with a shallow layer of leaf litter. This is produced from the leaves that fall from the trees throughout the year. The leaf litter is broken down by many insects that feed on it and it also decomposes quickly in the humid atmosphere. The thin layer that remains on the ground provides ideal growing conditions for all kinds of fungi. Some are shaped like parasols, some like glass threads, and some are even luminous.

**Left** *The dark, damp conditions due to lack of sunlight encourage the growth of fungi like this South American variety.*

**Below** *The crowns of the trees in the canopy grow close together, sometimes broken by an emergent tree.*

## Adaptations of rain forest trees

Rain forest trees look and behave quite differently from most other trees in the world. Unlike trees that grow in the temperate or subarctic zones, those of rain forests are not exposed to seasonal changes. Therefore they may flower, produce fruit or seeds, and shed leaves at any time of year. Rain forest trees are called broad-leaved evergreens. Their leaves are specially designed to repel rainwater, which falls on them at regular intervals. They have a waxy covering and a pointed "drip tip" that allows rainwater and fallen seeds to run off, thus keeping the leaves clean and dry.

The vast trees of rain forests use various means to support their immense weight. Some, like palms, have stilt roots growing down from their trunk or branches. Many of the largest trees have solid buttress roots growing from their bases to give them a broader-based support.

Every so often a giant forest tree falls down, creating a large gap in the canopy, through which sunlight can reach the forest floor. This encourages the sudden growth of seeds lying dormant in the leaf litter. Soon a number of seedlings will be rapidly growing. In time, the fastest-growing one or two will fill the gap in the canopy and blot out the sunlight once more.

*A beautiful rain forest orchid.*

## Rain Forest Plants

Rain forests contain many interesting plants. Climbers, such as lianas, grow like thick rope between the trees. Mosses and lichens grow on the trunks and branches of the trees, thriving in the moist atmosphere. Some other plants, such as orchids and bromeliads, grow out of the bark. They are called epiphytes, meaning that they grow on another plant and obtain all their nutrients from the water and dead plant matter that falls on them from the canopy.

## Growing Rain Forest Plants

Some rain forest plants have become popular houseplants. These include bromeliads of various kinds and foliage plants such as weeping figs, Ficus, and benjamina. Many of the palms, hibiscus, and orchids sold as houseplants also originated in rain forests.

You can try to grow your own rain forest plants, such as oranges, lemons, and grapefruit. Simply plant a pip in some potting soil, adding a little water. Keep the container in a warm place out of bright light, and water it occasionally. After a while, the pip should germinate. Your plant may not bear fruit but it will produce lovely scented flowers.

**Opposite** *Rain forest trees are enormous compared with most other trees in the world. The photograph shows a giant tree growing in southeast Madagascar. Even its buttress roots far exceed this man's height.*

**Above** *The enormous Victoria regia water lily grows on the Amazon. Its large leaves can support a child's weight.*

**Below** *Rafflesia arnoldii is the largest flower in the world, measuring up to a yard across. Its enormous flowers smell of rotting flesh, which attracts flies to pollinate it. It is found in Indonesia where its future is uncertain.*

No two rain forests are exactly alike in the number and variety of species they contain. Those of South America tend to be richer in plants than the forests of central Africa, while the Southeast Asian forests contain the greatest diversity of animal life. However, the basic pattern of layers is common to all rain forests, wherever they are. Moreover, the total number and variety of plants contained in rain forests is far greater than anywhere else. The forests of Panama in Central America have more plant species than are found in the whole of Europe. Although there are so many species, individual species are often found only in relatively small areas and in small numbers. This makes them particularly vulnerable when forests are extensively cut down.

The rain forests of the three main regions contain many kinds of primates. The South American spider and woolly monkeys have long prehensile tails to help them swing from branch to branch as they travel through the treetops. Below them tiny tamarins and marmosets live in the lower levels of the understory. Africa's rain forests contain a similar diversity of primates, the various species inhabiting different levels of the forest. The largest, like gorillas, are too heavy to live in the canopy and spend most of their time moving around and feeding on the ground.

Chimpanzees, on the other hand, live at both ground level and in the trees.

Madagascar's remaining forests are the home of the lemurs. These are primitive primates that are the ancestors of modern monkeys. They survived mostly on Madagascar when it became separated from the African continent. The rain forests of Southeast Asia are rich in primates, too. They include the small and agile apes called gibbons and the solitary orangutan, which is found only in the forests of the Indonesian islands Borneo and Sumatra.

## Rain Forest Monkeys in Danger

### GOLDEN LION TAMARIN

| | |
|---|---|
| Habitat | Tropical forests on Atlantic coast of southeast Brazil. |
| Population | Less than 100 animals. |
| Threats | Rain forest destruction. |
| Conservation measures | Protected in Poco d'Anta Reserve. 30 tamarins released into wild following captive breeding plan in London Zoo. |

### COTTON-TOP TAMARIN

| | |
|---|---|
| Habitat | Tropical forests of Colombia. |
| Population | Estimated small. |
| Threats | Forest habitat destroyed. 40,000 cotton-tops exported for pet trade and biomedical research. |
| Conservation measures | All primate exports from Colombia banned since 1974. Two reserves established. Captive breeding programs have bred several hundred cotton-tops. |

Other mammals also live high in the trees. The sloths of South America hang upside down under branches, suspended by the hooklike claws of their feet. As its name suggests, a sloth is a very slow-moving creature. It often blends in with its leafy surroundings by having a growth of greenish algae on its fur. Tamandua anteaters also inhabit the South American rain forest. Anteaters often climb up trees to feed on ants or termites, using their prehensile tails to grasp the branches.

Some rain forest mammals travel from tree to tree by "flying." The flying squirrel has a thin membrane of skin along the sides of its body. It jumps from one tree to the next, using the membranes between its outstretched legs to help it glide through the air. Dusk is the time to see flying foxes. These are really large fruit-eating bats of Southeast Asia. During the daytime they rest suspended from branches, and become active in the evening, when they feed on the fruiting trees in the forest.

*The understory of the Southeast Asian rain forest is home to this flying lemur.*

Left **Tarsiers are nocturnal creatures of the Indonesian rain forests. They mainly feed on insects, such as this cicada.**

Right **Tapirs are smaller relatives of the rhinoceros. They are found in the rain forests of both South America and Southeast Asia. The photograph shows the endangered Malaysian tapir.**

The secondary layer of the forest also has its own mammal inhabitants. There are various small climbing species such as the American possums, the Australian opossums, and the African bushbabies. They spend much of the day asleep, usually inside hollows in the trunks of trees. After dark they emerge to feed on insects.

The bareness of the forest floor discourages many larger mammals from living there. Small rodents like mice and agoutis of South America make their homes in the shelter of hollow logs and under shrubs. In Africa tiny antelopes called duikers nibble the fallen leaves of the forest floor. Larger mammals tend to be solitary like the okapi,

a very secretive and smaller relative of the giraffe, which inhabits the rain forests of central Africa. The Amazon forests and those of Southeast Asia both contain tapirs, which are smaller relatives of the rhinoceros. They are one of the species that provides evidence of the original land link between all the rain forests. Several species of cats inhabit rain forests. Best known are the jaguar, margay, and ocelot, which range from Central to South America, and the leopard cats of Southeast Asia. All of these cats are accomplished tree-climbers, although they spend most of the time on the ground.

*The South American margay is endangered through habitat loss and hunting.*

**Above** *Hummingbirds feed on the nectar of rain forest flowers and pollinate them.*

Over half the mammals that live in rain forests are found high up in the canopy. This is also the home of many species of birds, which are attracted by the abundance of fruits and seeds. When a forest tree is fruiting, it is visited not only by monkeys, fruit bats, and squirrels, but also parrots and hornbills or toucans. The parrot family is an extensive one and its largest and most brightly colored members, called macaws, live in the South American rain forests. Macaws have very

**Right** *Toucans live in the South American rain forests, feeding on fruits and berries.*

strong beaks for cracking open fruits and nuts. A flock of macaws provides a brilliant spectacle as it flies, screeching loudly, through a forest clearing. Toucans are another family of fruit-eating birds. They have enormous, boldly patterned beaks which they use to pluck fruits and berries from the trees. In the forests of Southeast Asia, hornbills live in a way similar to that of toucans in South America. Their heavy, flapping flight over the treetops is a familiar sight in almost any Asian rain forest.

The large fruit-eating birds, like parrots, toucans, and hornbills, all play an important role in maintaining the rain forest. Like some monkeys, they help to spread the seeds of the trees on which they feed. The birds swallow the fruits whole and then fly some distance before passing out the undigested seeds in their droppings.

Some birds help to maintain the forest in a different way, pollinating the forest trees by feeding on the nectar produced by their flowers. The tiny jewel-like hummingbirds of South America, and the sunbirds of Asia and Africa are all equipped with long, thin bills and tongues with which they sip nectar from flowers. Hummingbirds in particular have very rapid wingbeats that help them hover while they feed. In South America, hummingbirds are found not only in the hot, humid lowland forests, but also in cloud forests at high altitudes in the mountains.

The lower stories of the rain forest contain some of the most brilliantly colored birds on earth. The forests of New Guinea are the home of several species of birds of paradise. The males assemble together at clearings in the forest where they dance and show off their beautiful plumage, in order to attract the dull-colored females. South American cock-of-the-rocks, with their brilliant orange or scarlet plumage, are the New World counterparts of the birds of paradise.

Other birds live on the forest floor itself. The Asian forests are home to colorful peacocks and pheasants, and the jungle fowl, which is the

*Birds of paradise are among the most spectacular rain forest birds.*

ancestor of our farmyard hens. The South American rain forests contain large turkey-like birds called curassows.

Because so many rain forest species live in the canopy, the hunting animals of the forest concentrate their attention there, too. One of the most powerful hunters in the rain forest is an enormous eagle. Three different species exist, one in each of the three main rain forest areas. The monkey-eating eagle is found in Southeast Asia, the crowned eagle in Africa, and the harpy eagle in South America. All of them are very similar, swooping down into the canopy to grab birds, squirrels, and even monkeys in their immensely powerful talons. These eagles are the largest and most powerful predators of the rain forest canopy. They rear their young in nests in the huge emergent trees of the rain forest.

Tropical rain forests undoubtedly contain more species of birds than any other habitat. A typical small patch of rain forest may contain 400 species; by comparison in all of North America, 645 species of birds are found. In fact, the rain forests of Amazonia contain a fifth of all the bird species found in the world.

# More Unusual Creatures

Birds and mammals are the largest and best-known rain forest animals, but rain forests also contain a vast array of other creatures. These include reptiles and amphibians and so many different species of invertebrates that it is quite impossible to count them. All these smaller inhabitants occupy their own special areas in the forest, just like the mammals and birds.

Many of the snakes and lizards found in the rain forest are excellent climbers. Some of the snakes live high up in the canopy, climbing along branches and hiding among the leaves whose colors they closely resemble. Contrary to popular imagination, most snakes are small and thin. Living and hunting as they do high up in the trees, they would be at a distinct disadvantage if they were too large and heavy.

**Right**   *In the rain forest of Java, Indonesia, a flying lizard glides in midair. Its body flaps are spread to form "wings."*

**Below**   *The kingsnake lives on the ground. To avoid predators, its coloring mimics that of the poisonous coral snake.*

Some of the reptiles and amphibians that live in the forest canopy have developed special techniques for traveling from tree to tree. In Southeast Asia there are snakes, lizards, and frogs, that "fly" using the same technique as the flying squirrels. Flying frogs have very large webbed toes that act like tiny parachutes when the frog jumps into the air. Flying lizards have flaps of skin on the sides of their bodies. They can raise these flaps like sails to carry them through the air from one branch to another. Possibly the strangest aerial traveler of all is the flying snake. By flattening its body and coiling into an "S" shape, the snake can catch more air and glide downward from one tree trunk to the next.

The warm, moist conditions of the rain forest

*Frogs are found at almost every level in the rain forest. Many are especially adapted to live in trees. This red-eyed tree frog of Costa Rica lays its eggs on leaves.*

are perfect for the development of amphibians, like frogs and salamanders. Many of these creatures live in the rotting vegetation on the forest floor. But a number of frogs live in the trees, rather than on the ground. Some of these frogs have most unusual breeding cycles. They lay their eggs on leaves, and when the tadpoles hatch, the parent frogs carry them on their backs to the tiny pools of water contained in the leaves of bromeliad plants. Here each tadpole has its own nursery where it will grow to full size.

The invertebrate life of the rain forest is only now beginning to be studied. A single patch of forest may contain 40,000 different species. Most obvious are the butterflies, 150 species of which can be encountered in one piece of forest. They include some of the largest and most vividly colored in the world. The forest floor, with its carpet of dead and decaying leaves, and the moss-covered bark of the trees is the home of myriad beetles, ants, snails, millipedes, and spiders. Many thousands of species of insects have yet to be identified.

**Left** *This bird-eating spider is one of up to 40,000 species of invertebrates living in the same patch of rain forest.*

**Below** *A beautiful Costa Rican beetle.*

*Some of the world's most beautiful butterflies are found in rain forests. Many of them are endangered due to over-collection. This one is from Sierra Leone.*

Termites are particularly common on the rain forest floor since they can feed on dead plant tissue. Termites build enormous mounds in which they live. The mounds may be shaped like a toadstool or like a palace with many chimneys. Termites provide a major source of food for a great many rain forest species including frogs, lizards, birds, and mammals such as anteaters.

''A typical patch of rain forest, just 2.3 miles square, contains as many as 1,500 species of flowering plants, up to 750 species of tree, 400 species of bird, 150 kinds of butterfly, 100 different types of reptile, and 60 species of amphibian. The numbers of insects are so great that no one has been able to count them . . . but there may be as many as 42,000 species in this small area.''

United States National Academy of Sciences

# People and Rain Forests

So far we have looked at the astonishing variety of plants and animals that live in rain forests. We should not forget that people have also lived in rain forests for thousands of years, successfully using the forest materials to build their homes and using the plants as food and medicines.

Today about 200 million people live in rain forests. The South American rain forest is inhabited by various tribes of Amerindians, or American Indians. Pygmies and Bushmen live in

*The ancestors of these Pygmies have been living in the rain forest of central Africa for thousands of years, using local materials to build their homes and forest plants for food and medicines. Now their unique lifestyle is threatened.*

some parts of the African rain forests. Many different peoples live in the Southeast Asian rain forest, including some Pygmies in parts of the

Philippines, the Biami and Gibusi peoples of New Guinea, and the Sianh Daya in Borneo.

Each particular rain forest tribe has its own special traditions and beliefs, although all the original people's way of life is broadly similar. Traditionally rain forest peoples hunted wild animals and gathered seeds for food. Today many of them clear small patches of forest in which they grow food crops, such as maize, cassava, and sweet potatoes. Rain forest peoples have a special knowledge of the native forest plants, which they use as effective medicines to treat many ailments.

The unique way of life of rain forest peoples survived unchanged for thousands of years. It was first threatened when Europeans arrived in South America in the early sixteenth century and disturbed the peoples living in remote forest areas. At that time the number of Amerindians was about four million. Today their numbers have been reduced to fewer than 100,000. Earlier many Amerindians succumbed to European diseases. The numbers of African and Asian rain forest peoples have also declined over the centuries.

*The Amerindians of South America flourished in the vast rain forests of the Amazon basin, until the arrival of Europeans in the early sixteenth century. Today tribes still survive in remote rain forest areas. These Nahva Indians of Peru were first contacted by "outsiders" in 1986.*

**Left**  *Original peoples who inhabit rain forest regions are skilled at building homes from forest materials. This rain forest village is in New Guinea.*

**Below**  *Whole tribes of rain forest-dwellers have lost their ancestral homes and been forced to adopt new cultures. The new housing developments are a bleak alternative to traditional rain forest homes.*

## The price of "progress"

The rapid expansion of modern technology has particularly endangered rain forest peoples. When new roads are built through rain forests, once-remote areas become immediately accessible. Therefore it is easier to clear the trees to create land for farming or to build new settlements. Whole tribes of rain forest peoples

are driven away from their homes when outsiders arrive to clear and develop their patch of forest. Those who remain are forced to adapt to a very different way of life. For the first time they encounter different people bringing new religions and values, different methods of education, modern technology, new foods, and alcohol. They are exposed to different diseases, against which they have no natural immunity.

Many tribes have become extinct as a result of contact with other civilizations. About 87 groups of Amerindians formerly living in the Brazilian rain forest have been exterminated this century. In Indonesia millions of forest-dwelling peoples are being relocated far away from their homes in a

*How long will these Huli tribesmen in New Guinea be able to practice their traditions?*

government-sponsored project. Enormous numbers of people have been moved from the overcrowded islands of Bali, Java, and Madura to Irian Jaya, the Indonesian half of New Guinea. There they must adopt a completely different lifestyle.

In this chapter we have seen how the opening up of remote rain forest areas affects the traditional peoples living in them. In the next chapter we shall learn why rain forests are being destroyed so rapidly, and what other far-reaching consequences this may have.

29

There is no doubt that rain forests form the richest and most diverse habitat on earth. Yet rain forests are also suffering the most from the destructive influences of humankind. The world's rain forests are being cleared at an alarming rate.

---

*"At the present rate of destruction, all accessible tropical rain forests will have disappeared by the end of this century."*

Report of the United Nations

---

Every year 10–12 million acres are completely destroyed. This means that 30–50 acres disappear somewhere in the world every minute of every day. In addition, one animal species becomes extinct every half an hour.

All of the major rain forests are under similar attack. Until recently, Africa was losing its forests at the rate of 5 million acres a year, while in Southeast Asia, the remaining forests are disappearing at only a slightly slower rate. Central America now has only a third of the forest it used to contain thirty years ago.

Why are rain forests vanishing at such a tremendous rate? The answer lies in the needs of people, who cut down the forests in the belief that to do so will provide them with immediate benefits. In tropical countries where rain forests occur, most of the population outside towns and cities is engaged in small-scale farming. For these people, the forests have no obvious value, but cutting them down and clearing them away makes valuable farmland available. At the same time, the timber provides much-needed income

**This South American sawmill provides employment for local people, but does cutting down the forest make good sense?**

Estimated Area of Rain Forest by the Year 2000

| 1950 | 1975 | 2000 |

2400

1800

1200

600

area in millions of acres.

for most countries that possess rain forests. Some species of hardwood trees found in rain forests have a high commercial value. Teak and mahogany have fine, durable wood much in demand in the Western world for the manufacture of many products including furniture and boats. The less valuable trees can all be converted into pulp, plywood, and paper.

*A procession of logging trucks in Malaysia.*

*Modern machinery can cut down the forests at an alarming rate. Rain forests are disappearing wherever they stand in the way of progress.*

**Left** *Rain forests are destroyed so the ground can be mined for precious metals. Here manganese is being mined in Brazil.*

Nowadays, with modern technology the forests can be cut down more rapidly than ever. Heavy plant and machinery like bulldozers and cranes can clear large tracts of forest in a fraction of the time it used to take men using axes. There are more reasons for removing the forests, in addition to timber. Roads, dams, irrigation channels, canals, pipe and power lines are all increasingly needed in the developing countries. The forests that stand in their way are an inconvenient obstacle in the march of progress. Today, in a matter of a few months or a year, a large tract of rain forest can be converted into an enormous plantation or cattle ranch. It is grazing land for cattle that has replaced so much rain forest in Latin America, where beef farming is one of the main sources of revenue.

## The consequences of deforestation

It may seem sad but understandable that rain forests are destroyed to make way for the necessary growth and expansion in developing countries. Unfortunately, when the forests are cut down, they do not always provide suitable land for their new purpose. Rain forest soils are very old, and have supported countless generations of plant growth. They are poor in nutrients, which means that crops grown on them cannot prosper in the same way as the specially adapted native plants of the rain forest. When the forests are converted into farmland, they remain fertile for only a few years. Then more forest has to be cleared and the process repeated. The people who live in the forests know this, and employ a "slash and burn" method of agriculture, clearing a small patch of forest for temporary cultivation before moving on again. Now, however, this is happening on a gigantic scale, leaving vast areas of barren wasteland where crops and even grass fail to grow.

**Above** *The lifeless reality of an area of rain forest that has been burned down.*

**Left** *"Slash and burn" agriculture in a west African forest. This practice results in extensive areas being cleared, even though the land can only be used to grow crops for a very short time.*

deforested area

flooding

silting up

## Deforestation and Erosion

*Where rain forests have been cleared, erosion often occurs. Without the tree cover, rain cannot be absorbed and so it drains off the ground, gradually washing away the topsoil. Stripped of its nutrients, the remaining soil is of little value for growing crops. The soil that has been washed away causes rivers to become blocked with silt. When tropical rainstorms occur, the blocked rivers burst their banks, causing extensive flooding. Such floods have already occurred in South America and Southeast Asia.*

Removing the forest cover can have very serious side effects, too. Rain forests are directly responsible for local rainfall, since the giant trees absorb a great deal of rainfall that they slowly release as some additional moisture into the atmosphere. Cutting down the forests will reduce the rainfall of the region, eventually to the extent that desert conditions prevail. Stripped of its network of plant cover, the land is more prone to erosion. In turn, the soil eroded from the land can silt up rivers and lead to flooding. In India, severe flooding takes place annually in the river deltas, as a result of deforestation high in the Himalayan mountains. Forty years ago, almost half of Ethiopia was covered in forest, which provided vital water for crop irrigation. Today, only five percent of Ethiopia's forests remain. As a result of this, Ethiopia's enormous human population is prone to famine, drought, and floods.

*Soil erosion takes place as a direct result of cutting down the forests. These eroded hills are in Java, Indonesia.*

On a worldwide scale too, the consequences of rain forest destruction are far reaching. Rain forests are known to regulate global weather patterns. In tropical regions, over a billion people depend on the water generated by tropical forests to irrigate their crops. Even in the northern hemisphere, destruction of rainfall cycles and the build up of carbon dioxide in the earth's atmosphere are the likely results of large-scale tropical deforestation. Eventually this could lead to a general warming of the atmosphere called the "greenhouse effect" which itself could result in increased melting of the polar ice caps and subsequent rises in sea level.

*Soil erosion causes landslides, silting-up of rivers, and flooding, resulting in crop failures and national disasters.*

## Rainfall and Rain Forests

*Rain forests play a major role in regulating climatic conditions, especially rainfall. The huge trees draw up a great deal of water with their roots. Later the water is released as a vapor through the leaves in the process called transpiration. The evaporated water condenses into clouds in the atmosphere, to fall again as rain.*

*When large areas of rain forest are destroyed, the local water cycle is affected. Without the rain forests to store the water, serious droughts occur more frequently.*

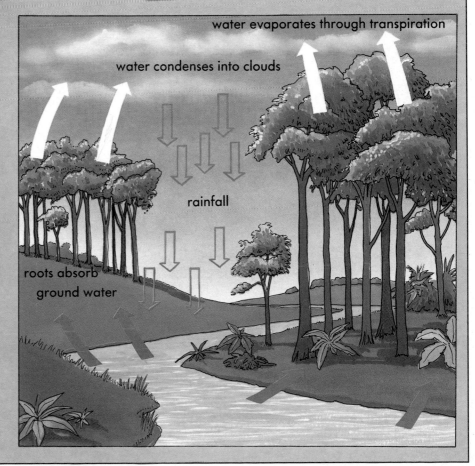

water evaporates through transpiration

water condenses into clouds

rainfall

roots absorb ground water

Once a rain forest has been destroyed, it cannot be replaced. Even if only the larger trees are removed, the fragile ecosystem will be destroyed. In the process, a unique community of plants and animals will be lost forever. Many of them are of immeasurable value to people. For centuries, people who live in the rain forests have used the chemical compounds of many plant species as drugs and medicines. Now the value of these herbal remedies has been recognized by modern science, too. Curare, ipecac, wild yam, and Madagascar periwinkle are just a few examples of plants whose compounds are used to fight major diseases such as cancer, leukemia, muscular and heart diseases. They also form the basic ingredients of birth control hormones, stimulants, and tranquilizing drugs. Possibly the best known drug originating from a rain forest plant is quinine. Quinine comes from the bark of a South American tree, the cinchona or "fever bark" tree. It has proved to be a very effective cure for malaria.

Rain forest plants are equally vital to agriculture and industry. Tea, coffee, bananas, oranges, lemons, peanuts, pineapples, and guavas are all native rain forest plants. Over half the grains

*Local peoples have always used plants as medicines. Now science has discovered the value of rain forest plants.*

*Many fruits and grains which form part of our staple diet are derived from rain forest plants. The South American passion flower is a popular plant in gardens today, while the fruit is widely imported to be used in cooking.*

eaten by humans, including rice and corn, originated in the rain forest. Industry, too, has already benefited greatly from rain forest products. Most famous is the rubber industry, dependent on a tree that grows wild in the rain forests of South America and Southeast Asia. Other industrial products such as resins for paints, oils, waxes, soaps, and plastics have also been produced from rain forest plants. Undoubtedly other materials having similar valuable properties remain to be discovered, but only providing there are still rain forests left in which to find them.

Today 40 percent of the world's rain forests have already vanished. The remaining forests are still being cut down at such a rate that some countries will have lost all their forests by the year 2000. However, before it is too late, efforts are being made to halt this drastic loss and conserve at least some of the unspoiled forests.

*Rubber is an important rain forest product. In the photograph a Brazilian woman collects latex from a tree.*

## How can we halt the destruction?

Most rain forests are found in the developing countries — the economically poorer countries. It is very easy for the richer, Western nations to criticize developing countries for destroying rain forests. However, in the process of "civilization" the more advanced industrial nations of the West have also sacrificed much of their own natural heritage. Today industrial countries continue to destroy and pollute the world's natural resources. They have certainly not set a good example for the developing countries to follow.

The Western world must share with the developing countries the responsibility of trying to conserve the remaining rain forests before it is too late. The Western nations can offer great expertise in biology, agriculture, forestry, and other fields that are relevant to the situation facing our rain forests today.

How can we stop the destruction of tropical rain forests? It is difficult, but there are several possible ways in which the felling of these magnificent forests might be brought under reasonable control. If current methods of agriculture were changed, this would reduce the continual need for land and, therefore, slow down the rate at which the forests are felled. Because the soils of rain forests are ancient and, therefore, poor in nutrients, they cannot sustain annual grain crops successfully. However, some crops can be beneficial to rain forest soils, for example various types of palms. These trees thrive naturally on the soils in the understory of the forest. As they grow into mature trees, palms help to stabilize the soil. So erosion is prevented while palm nut oil provides a useful source of income. This is not a simple answer for every area of rain forest in the world. However, it demonstrates that it is possible to grow profitable crops without using the shifting method of agriculture that is so disastrous for the forests.

**Right**  *Palm trees thrive naturally in the rain forest understory. Where forests have been cut down, oil palms can be grown. They produce palm nut oil and they help to stabilize the unprotected soil.*

*Selective logging means that only some trees, not the whole forest, are cut down. Gradually the forest will regenerate, just as it does when a huge tree naturally crashes down. This photograph was taken in the Victoria Falls rain forest, Zimbabwe.*

Another threat to rain forests that must be resolved is timber felling. Clear cut felling, in which all the large trees of the forest are cut down, certainly means the end of the forest. Selective logging is a less harmful alternative, in which timber can be harvested without destroying entire forests. Here only certain trees are removed at one time. Over the years new tall trees grow and fill the gaps, just as they do when a gap in the forest canopy is created naturally.

The timber industry causes further problems. It entails the creation of roads and tracks into the forest, so that the timber can be transported. The dragging away of tree trunks also harms the forest. If such damage could be avoided, and if selective logging were widely introduced, the prospects of rain forests would be brighter.

Ideally, however, timber felling needs to be halted entirely to guarantee the long-term protection of a rain forest.

## Practical measures

Recently, scientists have begun studying the forest canopy, using ropes and aerial walkways to take them high into the trees. Studying the life of the forest canopy will improve our overall knowledge of the rain forest ecosystem, but it does not help to stop the forests from being destroyed. In any case, some forests will have disappeared before the plants and animals they contain have been fully described by science.

Fortunately, the plight of the remaining rain forests has become the focus of international

concern in recent years. Conservation organizations like the International Union for the Conservation of Nature (IUCN), the World Wide Fund for Nature (WWF), and Friends of the Earth (FOE) have been successfully drawing people's attention to what is happening in the rain forests. Campaigns have also been mounted to try to protect specific areas, and also some of the most highly endangered rain forest animals, such as many species of primates.

**Left**   *A rain forest rally in Sydney, Australia. Northern Australia has its own extensive rain forests, some are under threat from cattle and sheep ranchers. Shown below is Middle Gorge, Queensland.*

*An Amazonian saman, or "rain tree" in bloom. Its future survival depends on the successful conservation of the South American rain forests.*

## Regrowing a Rain Forest

In northern Costa Rica, Central America, there is a special area of rain forest called dry forest. The trees that grow here are very rare and are now preserved in a small national park called Santa Rosa. An American botanist, Dr. Dan Janzen, would like to see the trees cover a much wider area, and has devised an ingenious way of doing this. His plan, which is being supported by the Costa Rican government, the Worldwide Fund for Nature, and many local landowners, is as follows:

Cattle from nearby farmland are allowed to graze in the national park and wander back onto their farms. At the same time, local farmers are encouraged to let the wild animals of the national park (for example,

tapirs) roam onto their land. In this way, the seeds of the rare dry forest trees that the cattle and the wild animals have eaten are transported by the animals and passed out in their droppings onto the farmland. Eventually, it is hoped the seeds will become trees that the farmers can use selectively for fuel. There would still be enough room for grazing land between the new trees on the farmland areas.

It is planned that the existing national park and the new dry forest area will combine to form a much larger national park called Guanacaste. This is the name of a well-known species of dry forest tree that used to flourish all along the Pacific coast of Central America.

A project designed to conserve a rain forest normally has several different aims. First, it must establish or strengthen protection for the area. This may involve persuading the government of the country to give it the status of a national park or reserve. It is also necessary to train people to act as guards or forest rangers, to protect the rain forest and its animals from poachers. Scientific surveys of the plants and animals will be required, to find out which are in most urgent need of protection. Finally, local people need to be made aware that the rain forest area is under protection. They should also be told the benefits of leaving it intact. Without their understanding and goodwill, the success of the venture is far less likely.

All of these factors require equipment, personnel, and time, which in turn cost a great deal of money. Until recently, funds for conservation work came directly from public donations together with a proportion of money from the governments concerned. Recently, however, a number of industrial companies, both large and small, have become involved in the crusade to save the disappearing rain forests. They are sponsoring projects that are carried out jointly with the conservation organizations.

The Jaguar car company is involved with the creation and maintenance of forest reserves in South America, which are the home of the large spotted cat that is the company's emblem. The forests of the Manu National Park in Peru and the Tortuguero National Park in Costa Rica have been further protected by grants for industry. Manu National Park actually contains 10 percent of all

## Rain Forest Conservation Projects Sponsored by WWF and IUCN

| | | | |
|---|---|---|---|
| Belize | Management of howler monkey sanctuary. | India | Management of the nine tiger forest reserves established since 1973. |
| Brazil | Project to improve rain forest conservation education. | Indonesia | Study of the medicinal use of plants in the forests of Siberut, near Sumatra. |
| Brazil | Reintroduction of golden lion tamarin. Management of reserves for endangered bird species. | Madagascar | Management of Beza-Mahalaly Forest Reserve. Training of local students. |
| Cameroon | Creation of Korup National Park. | Malaysia | Protection of Sumatran rhinoceros and orangutan. |
| Chile | Collection and propagation programs for rare rain forest plants. | Peru | Manu National Park created 1968 to protect jaguar, ocelot, giant otter, and Brazilian tapir. |
| Colombia | Prevention of poaching in Cahuinari National Park. | | |
| Ecuador | Management of coastal forest in Machalila National Park. | Rwanda | Prevention of gorilla poaching. |

bird species found in the world! In the Central American country of Belize, the giant multinational Coca-Cola company has donated a large area of land for the creation of a new rain forest reserve. Perhaps some other companies will follow this example.

Across the Atlantic Ocean in central Africa, a number of other projects are under way. The Korup Forest of Cameroon was the subject of a television documentary. Now it has been turned into a national park and several European companies, including the Midland Bank are helping to meet the expenses of its upkeep. Korup is believed to contain the most species of plants so far discovered in an African rain forest. Elsewhere

*The jaguar is the largest predator in the rain forests of Central and South America. Hunted extensively in the past for their skins, these cats are now safe in reserves sponsored by the car manufacturer, Jaguar.*

in central Africa, industry is helping to finance studies of gorillas and chimpanzees in Gabon, and the conservation of the forest home of mountain gorillas in Uganda. The Italian carmakers, Fiat, are sponsoring various conservation projects to protect the lemurs of Madagascar. This island country's few remaining patches of rain forest are the only home available for these remarkable primates.

## Korup National Park, Cameroon

Korup contains a quarter of all Africa's primates, 250 species of birds and 400 species of trees. Many of Korup's animals, including elephants and leopards, are at risk from hunters, who earn a living by selling animal skins. In March 1988 the Cameroon Government and WWF agreed on a plan to save the Korup rain forest, while at the same time providing income for the local people. Under the plan, a ''buffer zone'' was created around the precious rain forest. Here the local people may grow crops and timber, manage fish farms, and breed animals for hunting. This unique project may be a model for similar plans in other countries.

**Above**  *In the buffer zone around Korup, tree nurseries have been created to provide fast-growing timber for local people.*

**Left**  *Korup is Africa's richest remaining rain forest.*

The forests of Southeast Asia are equally important. Here, the British stationers, W. H. Smith, and the publishers, Batsford, are providing money to help conserve large mammals like tigers, rhinoceroses, and elephants that inhabit the rain forests of Indonesia. In southern China, a management plan is being developed to protect the rain forests in the Xishuangbanna Reserve.

Another by-product of the rain forest that until recently, has been overlooked, is tourism. Now several countries are looking to tourism as a way of making their remaining forests pay. Successful tourism means the forests are saved from the axe or chainsaw, and their animal inhabitants safeguarded. However, tourism depends on people's willingness to travel long distances to see for themselves what a rain forest is like. Already in the central African countries of Rwanda and Zaire, the endangered mountain gorillas of the rain forests have successfully attracted tourists. In learning about the gorillas, visitors also learn about the forests as a whole. So tourism not only provides much-needed revenue, but also the chance to show people why the conservation of the forest is vital.

*Rwanda's mountain gorillas have become a popular tourist attraction, and a flourishing asset to the country's economy.*

These are just a few examples of the tremendous efforts now being made to protect our rain forests. For some areas help may already be too late. An example is the rain forest of Brazil, which contains some of the world's rarest primates. Elsewhere, it seems that we have a good chance to save some of the remaining rain forests. If we do succeed, we then have to make sure that what is left of this unique environment is kept intact for the future. This is the only way to safeguard the magnificent array of plants and animals that live in rain forests throughout the world.

## How Can You Help?

The current rate of rain forest destruction is alarming, and it is easy to feel depressed by it. However, as you have been reading, much work is being done to preserve rain forests and protect their unique wildlife.

You can do your part by finding out as much as possible about what is happening to rain forests. You can help by talking to your friends and relatives about rain forests, and telling them why they are so important to us.

Above all, you can help by joining an international conservation organization. Many of them are listed on page 47. By becoming a member, you will be supporting the funds of the organization, and thus helping them to do their valuable work in preserving rain forests for all of us.

"The loss of tropical rain forests is the most crucial ecological issue of our time."

Catherine Caufield, author of *In the Rain Forest.*

# Glossary

**Altitude** The height of a place above sea level.

**Amphibious** Having the ability to live both on land and in the water, like frogs and newts.

**Botanist** A person who studies plants.

**Camouflaged** Colored or shaped to blend in with the surroundings.

**Deciduous** Plants whose leaves are shed once a year, normally at a particular time.

**Decompose** Rot away, decay.

**Dormant** In a state of deep sleep or inactivity.

**Ecosystem** A community of plants and animals and the environment in which they live.

**Equator** An imaginary line around the center of the earth, between the North and South Poles.

**Erosion** The wearing down of land by the action of wind and water, which gradually removes the soil or rocks.

**Evergreen** Plants with thick, waxy leaves that are not shed at regular intervals.

**Fauna** All the animal life of a given place.

**Flora** All the plant life of a given place.

**Habitat** The natural home of particular plant and animal species.

**Herbivorous** Feeding on plants.

**Invertebrates** Animals without backbones.

**Mammal** A warm-blooded animal with hair or fur on its body, whose young are fed on milk.

**New World** The continent of America which was so-called by Europeans after they claimed to discover it.

**Nutrients** Organisms that provide nourishment for the growth of plants or animals.

**Old World** That part of the world (Europe, Asia, and Africa) that was known before the so-called discovery of the Americas by Europeans.

**Poaching** Illegally catching and killing animals for food and other products.

**Pollute** To poison the land, water, or air with chemical waste and factory smoke.

**Predator** An animal that hunts another animal.

**Prehensile** Having the ability to coil up the tail and use it as a fifth limb.

**Primates** A type of mammal typically having flexible hands and feet with opposable first digits. Monkeys, apes, and humans are primates.

**Species** A group of animals or plants, different from all other groups, that can breed together to produce young, which can also breed together.

**Sponsor** A person or company that gives money to support an organization.

**Tropics** The area of the world situated between the Tropic of Cancer and the Tropic of Capricorn.

**Vegetation** All the different species of plants, including trees, that grow together in one area.

# Picture Acknowledgments

The photographs in this book are by: Ardea London Ltd 4, 6; David Bowden/WPL 40; Bruce Coleman Ltd *Cover* (Gerald Cubitt), 5, 7, 8, 16 left, 17, 19 above, 21, 22 above and below, 24 below, 28 main picture, 29, 31, 32 above and below, 34, 35, 36, 38, 39, 45; ICCE 41 below, 44 below; Frank Lane 16 right; Oxford Scientific Films 13, 14, 15, 18, 19 below, 20 above, 23, 33 above and below, 37, 40 below, 44 below; Tony Morrison 10, 13 below, 15 above, 20 below, 24 above, 27, 28 inset, 30, 43; WWF/UK 44 above. The illustrations are by Brian Watson.

# Further Reading

Attenborough, D. *Life on Earth* (Little, Brown, 1979).

Attenborough, D. *The Living Planet* (Little, Brown, 1984).

Forsyth, A. and Miyata, K. *Rain Forest Ecology — Central America* (Scribner, 1984).

Forsyth, A. and Miyata, K. *Rain Forest Ecology — South America* (Scribner, 1984).

Johnson, Sylvia *Animals of the Tropical Forests* (Lerner, 1976).

Nations, James D. *Tropical Rainforests* (Watts, 1988).

## Magazines

*National Geographic*
*Natural History* (American Museum of Natural History)
There are also many superb television documentaries about rain forests and their fascinating wildlife.

## Useful Addresses

Conservation Foundation
1250 24th St., N.W., Suite 500
Washington, D.C. 20037

The Environmental Defense Fund
Dept. P, 257 Park Ave. South
New York, N.Y. 10010

Friends of the Earth
1045 Sansome Street
San Francisco, Calif. 94111

Friends of the Earth Foundation
530 Seventh St., S.E.
Washington, D.C. 20003

Greenpeace
1611 Connecticut Avenue, N.W.
Washington, D.C. 20009

Greenpeace
2623 West 4th Avenue
Vancouver B.C. V6K 1P8
Canada

Sierra Club
730 Polk Street
San Francisco, Calif. 94109

## Places to Visit

### Zoos
Most zoos have some rain forest animals, including lemurs, monkeys, and wild cats. Some zoos have breeding programs for rare rain forest animals. The Central Park Zoo in New York City has an excellent example of a rain forest environment.

### Tropical bird gardens
Here you can see brightly colored rain forest birds, such as parrots and toucans. Some gardens have special tropical houses where hummingbirds fly freely.

### Butterfly farms
Most of these have heated glass houses where you can see beautiful tropical butterflies flying freely.

### Botanical gardens
Many gardens contain hothouses where rain forest plants and trees can grow. Two excellent examples are the Missouri Botanical Gardens in St. Louis and the New York Botanical Garden in The Bronx, New York.

# Index